CHOPIN

Preludes, Opus 28

An Authoritative Score

Historical Background

Analysis · Views and Comments

NORTON CRITICAL SCORES

BACH   **CANTATA NO. 4**
edited by Gerhard Herz

BACH   **CANTATA NO. 140**
edited by Gerhard Herz

BEETHOVEN   **SYMPHONY NO. 5 IN C MINOR**
edited by Elliot Forbes

BERLIOZ   **FANTASTIC SYMPHONY**
edited by Edward T. Cone

CHOPIN   **PRELUDES, OPUS 28**
edited by Thomas Higgins

DEBUSSY   **PRELUDE TO "THE AFTERNOON OF A FAUN"**
edited by William W. Austin

MOZART   **PIANO CONCERTO IN C MAJOR, K. 503**
edited by Joseph Kerman

MOZART   **SYMPHONY IN G MINOR, K. 550**
edited by Nathan Broder

SCHUBERT   **SYMPHONY IN B MINOR ("UNFINISHED")**
edited by Martin Chusid

SCHUMANN   **DICHTERLIEBE**
edited by Arthur Komar

STRAVINSKY   **PETRUSHKA**
edited by Charles Hamm

Frédéric Chopin

PRELUDES, OPUS 28

An Authoritative Score
Historical Background
Analysis · Views and Comments

Edited by

THOMAS HIGGINS

NORTHEAST MISSOURI STATE UNIVERSITY

W · W · NORTON & COMPANY · INC · *New York*

FIRST EDITION

Library of Congress Cataloging in Publication Data
Chopin, Fryderyk Franciszek, 1810–1849.
      24 preludes, op. 28.
      (Norton critical scores)
      Bibliography: p.
      1. Piano music. 2. Chopin, Fryderyk Franciszek,
1810–1849. Preludes, piano. I. Higgins, Thomas, ed.
II. Series.
M25.C   786.4   73–15982
ISBN 0–393–02161–0
ISBN 0–393–09699–8 (pbk.)

1 2 3 4 5 6 7 8 9 0

Contents

Preface   *vii*

Historical Background   *3*

The Score of Twenty-four Preludes, Op. 28

    The Score   *11*
    Textual Note   *57*

Analysis

    Thomas Higgins · Notes Toward a Performance   *61*
    Gerald Abraham · [Some Aspects of Chopin's Invention]   *72*
    Leonard B. Meyer · [Prelude No. 2]   *76*
    Charles Burkhart · The Polyphonic Melodic Line of Chopin's
       B-minor Prelude   *80*

Views and Comments

    Robert Schumann   *91*
    Franz Liszt   *91*
    Hippolyte Barbedette   *92*
    Frederick Niecks   *93*
    James Huneker   *93*
    George Sand   *94*
    Marcel Proust   *95*
    André Gide   *96*
    T. S. Eliot   *98*
    Kazimierz Wierzyński   *99*

Bibliography   *101*

Preface

In each of three centuries there were written for the keyboard great sets of Preludes—by Bach, Chopin, and Debussy, the latter two intended as musical tributes to their predecessors. Chopin's are the best known, and so widely loved as intimate pieces that T. S. Eliot could, in "Portrait of a Lady" express this truth in a cliché. Other writers paying tribute have included some of the greatest literary figures in this and the other century.

The "Views and Comments" in this volume were chosen to show points of view shared to a degree by the musician and the lay listener, by Chopin's champions and his critics. The idea that illness could be detected in the music—the grosser opinion included neurasthenia—was put forward by the Frenchman Barbedette, and was accepted in part by Schumann and George Sand. Gide denied it. The opinion of Chopin's biographer Niecks isolated and exaggerated Schumann's view of Op. 28 as "strange pieces . . . sketches, beginnings of Etudes." Ironically, the most accurate contemporary assessment of the Preludes is believed to have been intended as no more than flattery—but the comment that Marie d'Agoult wrote for Liszt's signature is now endorsed by posterity: "Admirable for their variety, the labor and learning with which they abound are appreciable only by the aid of a scrupulous examination; everything seems fresh, elastic, created at the impulse of the moment, abounding with that freedom of expression which is characteristic of works of genius." It is such "scrupulous examination" that the present volume is meant to assist.

Writings on the Preludes range in length from one-word descriptions ("pearls" is the noun most frequently encountered) to Chomiński's 347-page book in Polish, and in style from the effusive to the severe. Detailed analysis has been written for pianists (my dissertation, *Chopin Interpretation,* contains more than one hundred pages on the Preludes), for theorists, and for lay readers. Part of André Gide's essay is included here because its author was a great writer who loved Chopin's music and was a serious student of the piano all his life, but it must be said that his interpretations do not always square with the composer's intentions—which is the identical complaint Gide himself made about the performances of virtuosos in the twenties.

I am indebted to Dr. Ewald Zimmerman, musicological director of G. Henle Verlag, for permission to reprint his edition of the Preludes, which is the best published version available, and to the following persons in Warsaw: Professor Jan Ekier, Krystyna Kobylańska, Maria Prokopowicz of the National Library (who permitted me without reservation unlimited time with the Valldemosa autograph), Msgr. Wiktor Weinbaum and his staff at the Chopin Institute in the Ostragski Palace. In Paris I enjoyed the utmost cooperation and help from all the librarians I encountered at the Bibliothèque Nationale.

I am indebted also to Professor Edward Lowinsky for his new translation of Schumann's famous paragraph, to Jeanne Holland for preparation of the typescript, and for the patience and help of David Hamilton, music editor of W. W. Norton & Company.

Finally, I wish to thank my daughter, Kristin, for comparing some of my translations from the French with the originals, and, above all, to recall the devotion of my late wife, who accompanied me on research travels, aided my imperfect memory, and typed an earlier version of the manuscript. My own contributions to this book could not have been made without the generosity of an American Council of Learned Societies Fellowship, which enabled me to visit many of the institutions and persons mentioned above, and, more recently, to the American Philosophical Society for a summer research grant.

THOMAS HIGGINS

HISTORICAL BACKGROUND

Historical Background

Chopin dispatched the manuscript of his Preludes from Majorca in January, 1839, to his friend, copyist, and legman, Julian Fontana, in Paris: "I am sending you the Preludes. Recopy them, you and Wolff. I don't think there are mistakes.[1] You will give the copies to Probst [the agent for Breitkopf & Härtel] and the original to Pleyel."[2] To Camille Pleyel, the music publisher and piano manufacturer who had entered into an agreement with Chopin to publish his works, the composer wrote: "Dear friend, I finally send you my Preludes, which I've finished on your *pianino;* it arrived in the best possible state, despite the sea, the bad weather, and the Palma customs. I have entrusted Fontana to hand over to you my manuscript."[3] Two months earlier Chopin had written Pleyel: "My piano has not yet arrived. How did you send it? By Marseilles or Perpignan? I dream music but am not making any—because here there are no pianos . . . in that respect it's a barbarous country."[4] Two weeks after this letter, George Sand wrote to their friend Gryzmala: "Being without the piano bothers me very much for the youngster's sake. He rented a local make which irritates him more than it relieves. Nonetheless he is working."[5] It was the arrival of the long-awaited Pleyel upright in the middle of January that enabled Chopin, who was always

1. There were a few.
2. *Correspondance de Frédéric Chopin,* coll., rev., ann. and transl. by Bronislas Édouard Sydow in collaboration with Suzanne and Denise Chainaye, Paris, n.d., II, 287. Original in Polish.
3. *Corr. de F. Chopin,* II, 291, 292. Orig. French.
4. *Corr. de F. Chopin,* II, 271. Orig. French.
5. *Corr. de F. Chopin,* II, 273. Orig. French. In letters to Grzymała, who was seventeen years older than Chopin, George Sand, six years the composer's senior, habitually referred to him as "le petit."

extremely conscious of a piano's quality, to finish and test his Preludes in a matter of days.

The Preludes had been in the works for some time. In 1836 Chopin had penned the little A major (No. 7) in Delfina Potocka's album. Hordyński believed they may have been begun as early as 1831.[6] Chopin's correspondence offers no clue, but the opus number Chopin assigned to the Preludes suggests that if the plan of joining twenty-four short compositions, each in a different key *à la* Bach, under a single cover was perhaps conceived earlier, the actual work was not begun until late 1835 or early 1836. One cannot know how far along the Preludes were when Chopin arrived on the island in November, 1838, or how much new work had to be done. An autograph dated Palma, November 28, bears sketches of the A-minor (No. 2) and E-minor (No. 4) Preludes, and two other pieces in C-sharp minor and B-flat, which bear no resemblance to the Preludes in those keys. These sketches have been cited as evidence that at least four Preludes were written on Majorca—the A minor and E minor, plus Preludes in C-sharp minor (No. 10) and B-flat (No. 21) to replace the presumably rejected compositions in those keys.[7]

It is usually fanciful to associate the nature of an art work with the accidental physical conditions that surround its composition, but in the case of the A-minor Prelude, a piece that baffled most critics, one may be right in doing so. The sketch was written in a house called "Son Vent" near Palma; George Sand wrote of the sounds they heard in this place:

> In Majorca the silence is deeper than anywhere else. The asses and mules who pass the night at pasture interrupt it sometimes by shaking their bells. . . . The bolero too sounds forth in the most deserted places and on the darkest nights. No peasant is without his guitar, which he plays all hours. From my terrace I also heard the sea, but very far away and faint. . . .
>
> From a neighboring farm I heard the wail of an infant, and his mother, to quiet him, singing a pretty tune of the land, very sad, very Arabic. . . . The pigs awoke and lodged their complaint in a way I can't describe, whereupon the *pagès*, the *paterfamilias*, awoke to the voices of his dear pigs as had the mother to the tears of her nursing baby. I heard him put his head out the window to rebuke the guests of the sty in a

---

6. Fryderyk Chopin, *24 Preludia, Faksylominawe Wydanie Autografow F. Chopina,* Kraków, 1951, Zeszyt I, XI. This date suggests that Hordyński may not have discounted the legend that the D-minor and A-minor Preludes were written in Stuttgart in Chopin's great state of distress on learning of the fall of Warsaw.

7. Maurice J. E. Brown, *Chopin: An Index of His Works in Chronological Order,* London and New York, 1960, p. 119.

magisterial voice. They understood very well, for they fell silent. Then the *pagès*, apparently to get back to sleep, began to recite his rosary in a mournful voice, which, as sleep came and went, faded out or revived like the distant murmur of waves.[8]

Between the time of the sketch and the finished manuscript, Chopin suffered greater inconveniences. George Sand recalled that the seasonal rain began and was soon

> . . . streaming throughout poorly sealed rooms. . . . Although it was not really that cold, never have I suffered more from cold: for us who are used to heat in the winter, this house without a fireplace was like a mantle of ice on our shoulders, and I felt paralyzed. We never could get used to the suffocating smell of the braziers, and our invalid began to suffer and to cough. In this moment we became objects of horror and fright to the population.[9]

The landlord expelled the supposedly consumptive Chopin and "by threatening, made us pay for the *plastering* and *redecoration* of the whole house, on account of the contagion of a cold." [10]

The party of Parisians repaired to an abandoned monastery in Valldemosa, high in the hills, where things were better for a while, but Chopin's illness, aggravated by conditions in the island and the attitude of the natives toward the foreigners, changed his feelings from enchantment with the setting to annoyance and exasperation, and even alarm and fright. Because of George Sand's harrowing account of a storm, the D-flat Prelude will forever bear the name of "The Raindrop" (but does this Prelude "cast the soul into a terrible dejection?").[11] The composition she described could have been any of the Preludes featuring repeated tones or a repetitive figure in the accompaniment—the B minor, the E minor (one of the "new" Preludes), or even the A-minor piece Chopin had worked on at "Son Vent" before the rains. Chopin's illness and the privations of the place eventually routed the party and they fled the island in March, months before they had planned to, but the sojourn had not been profitless. "With what poetry his music filled this sanctuary,

8. George Sand, *Un Hiver à Majorque,* Palma, 1968, pp. 58–59.
9. *Un Hiver à Majorque,* pp. 59–60.
10. *Un Hiver à Majorque,* p. 168. The italics are George Sand's. In a footnote to his translated and annotated edition of *Winter in Majorca* (Valldemosa, 1956), p. 48, Robert Graves wrote that "Majorcans still burn the bedding on which a consumptive has lain, fumigate the house and rub the bedstead with vinegar." There is in fact reasonable doubt that Chopin was suffering from the disease diagnosed on Majorca.
11. George Sand, *Histoire de Ma Vie,* Paris, 1902–04, pp. 439–40.

even during his most painfully agitated moods!" [12] Besides the Preludes, the composer finished the F-major Ballade, Op. 38; the Mazurka in E minor, Op. 41, No. 2; the Polonaise in C minor, Op. 20, No. 2; and began the Scherzo in C-sharp minor, Op. 39.

Acting on Chopin's instructions, Fontana copied Chopin's manuscript of the Preludes, then turned it over to Pleyel. Despite the dedication on the first page to J. C. Kessler (at whose musical soirées in Warsaw Chopin had performed as early as 1829), it was this manuscript that served as the basis for the first French edition, dedicated to Pleyel. The first German edition was eventually dedicated to Kessler. (In Chopin's frequent and well-documented rages during those months, over what he saw as skulduggery and double dealing on the part of agents and publishers, including Pleyel, he considered and reconsidered his dedications.)

Because of what seemed a close resemblance between Fontana's handwriting and Chopin's, the copyist's manuscript was taken in Germany for the master's. One of Fontana's copies of the A-flat Prelude passed through famous hands to repose in a great archive,[13] and facsimile pages of others were included in critical publications. (Even today, there is commercially available a framed facsimile of the first page of the D-flat Prelude, the buyer of which believes he has a reproduction of Chopin's manuscript, but it is only one of Fontana's copy.) The confusion of sources that makes such things possible is of more than passing interest, since Fontana's copy of the Preludes must be recognized as such if one is to make the better choice of a source for the score of Op. 28.

From Majorca the party of Chopin, George Sand, and her children went to Arenys de Mar, near Barcelona, then to Marseilles, then to Nohant, where Chopin wrote Fontana in August: "Pleyel wrote me that you are very obliging and have corrected the Preludes." [14] The composer did not return to Paris until October, by which time both the French and German editions were in print. When Chopin took the opportunity to correct proofs, he could introduce final changes in details, as adjustments in a tempo, the length of a slur, the precise point of a pedal release, the change of a pitch or a harmony. In such compositions, his autograph is

12. George Sand, *Winter in Majorca,* excerpt from *Story of My Life,* transl. Robert Graves, p. 174.

13. Gesellschaft der Musikfreunde, Vienna. (Earlier, it had been given to Brahms by Clara Schumann.)

14. *Corr. de F. Chopin,* II, 349. Orig. Polish.

a very valuable, but penultimate, source. In the case of the Preludes, however, the manuscript Chopin sent from Valldemosa, now in the National Library, Warsaw, must be considered the only authoritative source. Some of Fontana's copies were faithful, but in cases where they were not later seen and amended by Chopin, they must always rank beneath the autograph from which they were copied. Fontana's copy of the Preludes, unlike better ones he made of some other compositions, was not the faithful job the composer had a right to expect (yet nowhere in Chopin's correspondence is there a hint of reproof to his friend and factotum for his part in the publication of the Preludes). Furthermore, the first German edition, which had its source in this copy, faithfully reproduced the copyist's errors while neglecting to rectify Chopin's; in addition, it was evidently marred by the most ignorant and officious editing imaginable. A full catalogue of errors is beside the point here; one might say that only the little A-major Prelude seems to have been exempt. In addition to wrong notes, dynamics, and fingerings, one encounters imprecisely placed slurs, pedals and pedal releases, and even missing measures. As Chopin was returning to the mainland from Majorca, obliged to share sea accommodations with pigs, his Preludes were already subject to subversion. To name two examples, the omission of a pianissimo, a pedal, and a crescendo suppressed the character of the conclusion of the C-minor Prelude; while neglect of a *più animato* plus the mistaking of Chopin's letter "f," in a series of measures to be repeated marked "a.b.c.d.e.f.g.h.," for the dynamic letter *f* (for forte) denies the G-minor Prelude its thrust toward climax, and equally alters its character.

Certain post-publication original sources provide interesting footnotes to the score of the Preludes, such as the album autographs of the C-minor Prelude—one made for Alfred de Beauchesne,[15] the other for Anny Szeremetiew.[16] There are also the editions bearing Chopin's pencil marks, one which belonged to his sister Louise,[17] another to the Polish pianist and composer Napoleon Orda.[18] The former contains, among other details, Chopin's suggested fingering for the B-minor Prelude. The fullest of such sources available to scholars is the music used by Chopin's student Camille Dubois, which contains pencilled fingering for the F-major Prelude.[19] The pencil marks in the music of Chopin's pupil

15. Bibliothèque Nationale, Paris.
16. Lenin Library, Moscow.
17. Chopin Institute, Warsaw.
18. Chopin Institute, Warsaw.
19. Bibliothèque Nationale, Paris.

Jane Stirling, which so influenced the editor of the Oxford Complete Edition, were not made by Chopin alone, according to Krystyna Koby-lańska of Warsaw; unfortunately, Miss Stirling's seven volumes of first editions, now owned by Marthe Édouard Ganche at Lyon, were, on investigation, not available for study.

THE SCORE

24 PRELUDES

OPUS 28

ACKNOWLEDGMENT

This edition of Chopin's 24 Preludes, Opus 28, is reproduced by kind permission of G. Henle Verlag, Duisburg and Munich, Germany.

24 PRELUDES, OPUS 28

Brown-Index 124

II

Prelude 2

Brown-Index 123

Brown-Index 107

Largo

Brown-Index 123

4.

Allegro molto

Brown-Index 107

5.

Lento assai

Brown-Index 107

6.

Brown-Index 100

7. Andantino — *p dolce*

8. Molto agitato

Brown-Index 107

Allegro molto

Brown-Index 123

10.

Prelude 12

Brown-Index 107

poco ritenuto

Brown-Index 107

Allegro
pesante

Brown-Index 107

14.

Prelude 15

Sostenuto

Presto con fuoco

Brown-Index 107

Prelude 16

17.

Allegro molto

18.

cresc.

Prelude 18

Brown-Index 107

Brown-Index 107

20.

Brown-Index 123

21.

Molto agitato

Prelude 23

Brown-Index 107

24.

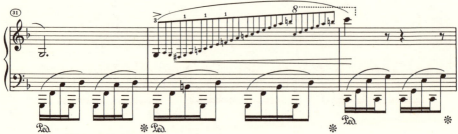

Textual Note

The editor of the musical text used here, Dr. Ewald Zimmermann, includes the following comments in the Preface to the edition, as explanation of his procedures and sources:

> The source material of the preludes is less complicated than that of the other work-groups. For Op. 28 there exists an autograph of all twenty-four preludes, which formed the basis of the original French edition, as well as a copy of this autograph which was made by Chopin's boyhood friend Fontana and which was used as basis of the first German edition. Later on in Paris, Fontana acted as copyist and was a loyal friend and helpmate to Chopin in the recurring complexities of daily life till his emigration to America in 1841. Besides these two primary sources, there are also autographs and manuscript copies of several individual works. . . .
>
> The notation follows essentially that of the sources and thus also optically reproduces tonal relationships which through the modern practice of systematically writing the notes of the right hand in the upper, and those of the left hand in the lower, staff are often lost in the printed music. Figures in italics stem from manuscript sources, or the first editions, and therefore represent the fingering which has been suggested by Chopin himself. The signs in parenthesis are not in the sources, where they evidently were only omitted inadvertently.

[The sources referred to are the following:
1) Autograph fair copy: National Library, Warsaw (facsimile edition published by Polish Music Publications, Cracow, 1951).
2) Fontana's copy of the autograph: Private collection.
3) First French edition: Ad. Catelin et Cie., Paris, 1839; based on Chopin's autograph.
4) First German edition: Breitkopf und Härtel, Leipzig, 1839; based on Fontana's copy.
5) First English edition: Wessel & Co., London, 1840; probably based on the first French edition.]

ANALYSIS

Unless specified otherwise, all numbered footnotes in the following essays are by the author.

THOMAS HIGGINS

Notes Toward a Performance
with References to the Valldemosa Autograph

Since composition and performance are inseparable, one is helped to discover the essence of a particular Prelude through close observation of Chopin's directions.

Prelude No. 1, C major

The crux is the degree of Agitato, not Molto agitato as in No. 22, but neither as calm as Gide's description: ". . . this work, in its entirety, is simply like a lovely, quiet wave . . . preceded by another and smaller wave, and the whole draws to a close in an eddying which dies out gradually." [1] One can, on the contrary, hear the "passionate breathing" Schumann described. Although the terrain is clearly mapped out, Chopin saw fit to leave the player latitude in the interpretation by certain omissions. There is no specific tempo with the Agitato (e.g., Allegro agitato). There are no specific dynamic levels after the *mezzoforte* opening until the piano in m. 25; none, therefore, in the climactic m. 21, and no degree of withdrawal from the crescendo and stretto. Chopin has also left the relative importance of the two melodic parts an open question.

Prelude No. 2, A minor

The division of the left hand into two parts is maintained in the notation for only two measures, but should be continued, with the inner part legato. The outer part may be lightly detached throughout, or else

[1] André Gide, *Notes on Chopin*, transl. by Bernard Frechtman, New York, 1949, p. 36.

only where the span is too great for the hand (the interval of a tenth on white keys was about one-eighth inch smaller on Chopin's Pleyel). Pedal is not needed, and the effect of the single pedaled measure is more telling if the pedal is avoided elsewhere. In compositions where he supplied a metronome rate, Chopin's lentos are somewhat faster than one expects.

In the autograph the diminuendo from m. 13 through m. 18 is written above the brace. The crescendo wedge and the *slentando* in m. 18 are written between the clefs. It is evident that the sound must be rather loud in mm. 12 and 13 if a true diminuendo is to last for six measures (except for the brief sign of growth in m. 16). A lento closer to andante than to adagio makes it possible.

The final chord might be arpeggiated from top to bottom rather than in the usual manner.

Prelude No. 3, G major

Chopin's character term Vivace—without the inclusion of a specific tempo range—leaves the player some latitude. Chopin's vivaces are not excessively fast, thus the "presto vivace" of some pianists seems inappropriately fast in this Prelude, which is clear, light, and unpedaled. An interesting and unusual break in slurring occurs between mm. 24 and 25 —between an appoggiatura and its note of resolution.

Prelude No. 4, E minor

At the head of this famous Largo (and nowhere else in the Preludes) Chopin wrote the word *espressivo,* relieving the narrow, keening melody and implacably descending chords. On most instruments in most acoustical settings, more frequent pedaling would be required than the two places he noted. Chopin's omission of directions for the pedal here and in Prelude No. 20 may have meant that its use, following harmonic changes, was so obvious as not to require notation. On the other hand, perhaps he did not wish to impose a prosaic pedaling in this Prelude, but rather to permit the performer to introduce subtle blurrings such as can be seen in Preludes Nos. 7, 13, and 21. Cortot wrote that Chopin's monastery cell at Valldemosa was "so resonant that the vibrations of his piano were amplified to . . . a jangle of sound," [2] which may have pre-

---

[2] Alfred Cortot, *In Search of Chopin,* transl. by C. and R. Clarke, New York, 1934, p. 64.

vented him from calculating such subtleties, but this theory seems unlikely when one looks at the next Prelude.

Prelude No. 5, D major

The most important instrument of expression here is the pedal, which effects groupings of consecutive notes into specific harmonies, outlines the figure in eighth notes, and in general relieves metrical angularity. In m. 29 it is depressed three times—the tempo is Allegro molto—yet in mm. 34–37, where a downward diatonic melody is featured, it is held through. On the other hand, there is no pedal at all in mm. 21–28. For some reason the original pedaling was altered in the "First Critically Revised Edition," which attempted to correct some of the many errors of the first German edition.

Prelude No. 6, B minor

A literal reading of the symbols produces the best effect. Pedal in the opening measures would turn the left-hand melody into commonplace harmony. Such a dissolution into harmony is desired in the chord on C major in m. 13 and the remembrance of the melody in m. 23.

The accents and short slurs in m. 1 should not be understood to continue further into the piece. In the autograph these signs are deleted in mm. 2–6 and mm. 11–18. Was this the Prelude to which George Sand referred? If so, Chopin may have deleted the signs in annoyance at her suggestion that he had been influenced by the sound of rain dropping on the roof.

Prelude No. 7, A major

Pedal is rarely used in the manner Chopin indicated: one usually hears a change on the second as well as the first beat in the odd-numbered measures, which is presumably made to keep the melody clear. The original pedaling should be preserved whether one plays on Chopin's piano or our own modern one, since in a tempo of Andantino the slight blur of ornamental tones in the *piano dolce* melody is pleasing, and (more important) the fundamental in the bass survives—a crucial value.

The indication for the thumb to strike both A-sharp and C-sharp in m. 12 enjoins one from the all-too-common arpeggiating of this chord.

Prelude No. 8, F-sharp minor

The constant dotted-eighth-plus-sixteenth rhythm of the melody, the similar ornamental shapes surrounding this melody, and the sixteenth-triplets-plus-eighth-note in the bass—all could turn this Prelude into a *moto perpetuo,* but posed against this is the Molto agitato, and especially the variety of short and long slurs that indicate exact punctuation and stress. While no slur begins off the beat, one sees slurs of one beat, two beats, four beats (one measure), two measures. (In the printed editions, and even in the autograph, there is sometimes doubt whether the slur terminates at the right margin or was meant to be carried over to the next line.) The short slurs tend to slow the action when a new period is ushered in (m. 8), or where the composer wished to separate the motives for a more emphatic expression. In contrast, at the dramatic return in m. 19 of the opening theme, Molto agitato e stretto, there is no new slur.

Prelude No. 9, E major

Chopin's notation here and in the *Polonaise-Fantaisie,* Op. 61, of a melody in dotted-eighths-plus-sixteenth-notes over a triplet figure recalls Baroque practice, in which the sixteenth note is played together with the third note of the triplet. In the autograph the notes are not only arranged one above the other, but sometimes have a common stem. By the same reckoning, the thirty-second notes fall exactly between the final triplet note and the following beat.

The very interesting asymmetrical slurs produce an anacrusis before m. 3, and following Chopin's characteristic practice, lengthen as the composition progresses.

Prelude No. 10, C-sharp minor

In order to give the second motif—repeated figure in a design—(mm. 3-4, 7-8, 11-12, 15-16, 17-18) its true mazurka-like gesture, it is necessary to observe the original pedaling: no pedal in these phrases, except one that adds resonance to the trill in m. 7. In this way the values of notes and rests survive, especially the important sixteenth rests in the left hand (m. 4, 8, 12, 16, and 18).

The rhythm in the opening motif is also like that of a mazurka—

sixteenth triplets followed by sixteenths—but the Allegro molto is so fast that the common dance is transformed into something like the whirling entrance of a ballerina.

Prelude No. 11, B major

The identical melodic fragment, recurring throughout this piece—in mm. 2–5, 6–9, 15–17 (but here lacking its first measure), 18–20 (lacking its final measure)—and forming the basis of the coda, is woven into the rest by Chopin's long slurs. In contrast, short slurs separate and make prominent the delightfully relieving climax (mm. 10–14). Another relief to the continuous motion of eighth notes is the opposition of rhythmic structure to the 6/8 meter—e.g., mm. 5 and 10 are "3/4."

Chopin's Vivace is buoyant and lively, but not the signal for a great rate of speed.

Prelude No. 12, G-sharp minor

Many details in this Prelude combine to produce a powerful imitation of mechanism—an almost perpetual motion of eighth notes, strong accents and dynamics, a texture of octaves and chords in the bass, a tempo of Presto. Nevertheless, Chopin's scheme of slurs in the opening eight measures introduces the semblance of a living, breathing struggle against the toccata elements. Elsewhere the slurs interrupt harmonic formulae (mm. 15–17, 18), bind the recapitulation to its preceding dominant link (m. 40), and outline a rhythmic structure that is in opposition to the barlines (mm. 65–73).

Prelude No. 13, F-sharp major

This Prelude is the only one featuring a second theme in a different tempo from the opening. Texture and key are changed as well, but the difference to the performer will not seem great because of the strong melodic character of both.

The original pedaling is more unusual here than in any other Prelude (except for places in Nos. 16 and 21), causing a considerable blurring of entire half-measures, usually at or near the end of syntactic phrases. The phrases themselves recall Proust's description (see p. 98).

Prelude No. 14, E-flat minor

Another *moto perpetuo,* but here the composer reveals the Prelude's character through a carefully wrought contour of dynamic wedges. There are no slurs, no pedals, and no change in the *pesante* articulation.

Unison passages in Chopin's music display a wide variety of character. There is the virtuoso Variation II in the youthful set on Mozart's *La ci darem la mano* (Op. 2), the dramatic recitative in the Larghetto movement of the F-minor Concerto, the more impetuous passages in the F-minor Prelude, and the chilling finale of the Sonata Op. 35, *sotto voce e legato,* of which Chopin wrote with characteristic understatement: "After the [funeral] march the left hand plays in unison with the right." [3]

Prelude No. 15, D-flat major

This Prelude is so familiar that every player is acquainted with its character. If the Prelude in F-sharp has a middle section in a contrasting tempo, the contrast here, without tempo change, is nevertheless much greater. A change in mode, register, texture, and dynamism make this long middle section a drama in itself. The pedal indications are almost entirely reserved for places where the hand needs its help to produce a legato—a point overlooked by many pianists.

It is perhaps understandable that in this familiar piece a cut is sometimes made of mm. 43–58, but this can only reduce the poignancy of the return to D-flat.

Prelude No. 16, B-flat minor

To present-day pianists, the most surprising instruction is that of pedal which covers forty-eight mostly stepwise notes in mm. 2–4 and 5–7, yet it is consistent with the composer's willingness in other places (e.g., Prelude No. 7) to blur ornamental or passing tones under a harmonically stable bass. The welter of sound resulting here is extreme even on a Pleyel of Chopin's time, and one is hard put to offer an adequate explanation. Perhaps the composer feared that a clearer projection of the left-hand rhythm would have turned this inexorably onrushing torrent into a dance. In the powerful fortissimo repeat, pedaling does not even remain

3 *Corr. de F. Chopin,* II, p. 348.

congruent with harmonic syntax, ignoring in m. 32 the entrance of the subdominant. There is no more extreme example of harmonic confusion and cacophony anywhere in Chopin's music.

Prelude No. 17, A-flat major

In the autograph, the composer's slurs promote a forward motion together with a sense of freedom through an unpredictable variety in length of poetic lines:

mm: 1 2 3 4   5 6 7 8 9 10   11 12   13 14 15 16 17 18

Later, slurs of one measure each (mm. 23, 24) punctuate the modulation by sequence. In the final version of this rondeau theme, from m. 65 on, the poetic action is static as slurs of 2 mm. length predominate until the long line from mm. 81 to 87.

An attractive blur of the appoggiatura B-flat with the tonic A-flat in m. 4 recalls the blurred end of the first phrase in Prelude No. 13.

Prelude No. 18, F minor

In the autograph one finds the "wedge" stress sign rather than the staccato mark in mm. 14, 15, and 17. (In the Henle edition reproduced here, these signs appear in mm. 9–12.)

In mm. 10 and 12 there is a temporary opposition, through dynamic wedges, in the course of a long crescendo. (See an opposite instance in Prelude No. 2, m. 16.)

Pedal has been absent in the unison passages but is brought in as energy toward climax is increasing (mm. 12 and 17).

The triple forte, as seen in m. 20, is Chopin's loudest mark, and does not occur often, especially after the early music written in Poland. One does not find it elsewhere in the Preludes except in No. 24.

Prelude No. 19, E-flat major

The rhythmic structure of this etude-like piece should not be deduced by analysis of its form alone, but also through a close observation of its dynamic contours. Although this Prelude begins with an anacrusis, one cannot sense that the final beats in mm. 4 and 8 are also anacruses, because the composer has made them ends rather than beginnings by the use of pedals lasting two beats and decrescendo wedges. Throughout, the player need only observe the legato and follow the course of the dynamic wedges, present in almost every measure, to project the movement in this prelude.

Passing tones in the melody are blurred in a few places, and in mm. 29–32 and 66–69 pedal combines with harmony to produce the effect of 2/4. The short articulating slurs in mm. 32 and 68 effect a continuation of the "2/4"; therefore, at the end a definite sense of the original meter is delayed until one hears the two final chords.

Prelude No. 20, C minor

In a note at the bottom of the autograph Chopin wrote a note for Pleyel: "note for the publisher of the rue Rochechuart: small concession made to Mr. XXX [4] who is often right." The concession was the repetition of mm. 5–8, but with the addition of a *pp* in m. 9, a "cresc." in m. 11, and a pedal under m. 12, presumably beginning with the last beat. In album versions of this Prelude made later, Chopin omitted these measures. Perhaps he regretted the "petite concession" and considered his original conception superior. It has classic simplicity, while the published version suggests a possible programmatic text.

In m. 3 there is a disputed E on the fourth beat, some editions, including the one in this volume, having E-flat. The evidence from sources is as follows:

1. The autograph sent from Majorca shows no flat.

2. The autograph in Alfred de Beauchesne's album, dated January 30, 1840, shows no flat. (There is a fortissimo in the final measure here.)

3. Chopin made no correction in the music of his pupil Camille Dubois when she studied this Prelude.

4. There is no flat sign pencilled into the music of Chopin's sister Louise.

5. The music of Jane Stirling had the flat pencilled in, but since this source is unavailable for study, one cannot verify that it was added by Chopin.

6. The English first edition has the flat, but it appears to have been added after the type was set.

[4] The French writer on music, François-Henri-Joseph Blaze (called Castil-Blaze), who as music critic of the *Journal des Débats*, 1822–32, had signed his articles "XXX."

7. In contrast with the first four sources listed above is the album autograph of Anny Szeremetiew, dated May 20, 1845, which has the flat sign.

Although Chopin sometimes omitted accidentals inadvertently, e.g., the naturals before the C's in Prelude No. 6, mm. 12 and 13, it is doubtful that he would not have rectified his omission on one of the other sources. The English edition and the Szeremetiew album autograph justify a legitimate alternate version post publication.

The only pedal indication is in m. 12, which binds the last beat to the chord of the final measure. Otherwise the legato nature of the composition calls for a change of pedal on each beat, which the composer may have considered too obvious for specific indication.

Prelude No. 21, B-flat major

The cantabile melody enjoys a small articulative break in m. 5, where a new slur creates an anacrusis, and again in m. 10, on the final sixteenth note. There are three simultaneous slurs in mm. 33 and 35, the topmost showing that the notes F–D and G–E each form a melodic phrase even if legato articulation is physically impossible.

Pedaling is very imaginative, and more unusual than in any other Prelude except perhaps No. 13. A short pedal beginning on the last beat of m. 12 extends through the beginning of the next measure, creating a dominant-seventh harmony on the phrase end and binding this phrase to the double-notes in octaves following. The long pedal in mm. 19–24 extended at first only to the end of m. 22, but the composer crossed out his release and new pedal in m. 23. Even in a forte passage he was not reluctant to blur a non-harmonic chord into its resolution. The almost diatonic figure in m. 47 is pedaled, but elsewhere one needs a good finger legato in both hands, especially for the long chains of melodic double-notes.

Prelude No. 22, G minor

Molto agitato is a description of the strong syncopations in the left-hand octave melody (inactive on the fourth beat), and its harmonic complement in the right hand (active on the second beat). But it is instruction as well that this dragging and pulling cannot be projected by a neat and precise alternation of hands in a smooth rendering of 6/8.

There is a strong thrust toward climax beginning in the repetition (mm. 25–31) of the eight-measure section in A-flat. The passage is already fortissimo, is marked *più animato* beginning in m. 30, and at m. 36 marked "cresc." which extends to the climactic augmented sixth chord three measures later. (Unfortunately the first German edition omitted the *più animato* and introduced a milder "forte" at this point.)

The final chord is rolled in the right hand, which suggests a softening that seems inappropriate, but can be understood if it was intended as a preparation for the next Prelude.

Prelude No. 23, F major

The running sixteenth notes, *delicatissimo,* the left-hand arpeggios and rolled chords, the two E-flats (in m. 12 and the famous one in m. 21) accented as though plucked—all suggest an apotheosis of the harp in this exquisite short piece.

The player should note this characteristic example of Chopin's slurring practice, in which four successive two-measure slurs are followed by a single long slur covering the remaining fourteen measures.

The tempo of Moderato calls for a slower pace than what one usually hears.

Prelude No. 24, D minor

In the opening measure a quarter-note A emerges from each of the two figures. The next eight measures are shown in the autograph by repeat signs, not notes. It is probable that similar quarter notes were intended throughout, as an addition to the texture and a pivot for the left hand.

The melody takes a breath in m. 4 immediately after the opening three-note motive, but when the theme is repeated in A minor, there is no slur break (m. 22). The sixteenth-note G in m. 38 is not an anacrusis, but the final tone in the link to the development. In contrast to Chopin's practice of binding sections together (Preludes No. 8 and 12), his slurs here call for a fresh start in m. 39, and the player may infer a dramatic pause between these measures.

Pedal undergirds the first climax, in m. 55, where the melody shatters in descending chromatic thirds. The second climax begins triple-forte in m. 61 and ends with three accented octaves in mm. 64–65. But the fury of the movement does not subside. In the last twelve measures, the headlong arpeggios alternate three times with separate three-note motives: in mm. 68–69; disguised as quintuplets in mm. 72–73; and doubly slowed in 75–77 to three great bell-claps. This third and final climax, beginning on the last beat of m. 73, is, like the first, also under-pinned by pedal.

The most important key to interpretation is the word *appassionato,* which in Op. 28 appears only here.

GERALD ABRAHAM

[*Some Aspects of Chopin's Invention*] †

Chopin's form is generally considered to be his weakest point. It was also the weakest point of all his contemporaries. And, of course, compared with Beethoven's—a fantastically unfair comparison—his sense of form is primitive, being limited almost exclusively to the possibilities of more or less modified ternary form. The elementary formula ABA is the structural basis of the vast majority of Chopin's shorter pieces. It underlies the majority of his second-period mazurkas, all his second-period polonaises, and practically all the second-period nocturnes. Its predominance in the études has already been mentioned—Nos. 1 and 3 of the Trois Nouvelles Études are the only exceptions—and it is either implicit or explicit in a number of the Preludes. Only the valses tend to break away into looser patterns akin to the 'suite of waltzes' initiated by Hummel in 1808 (*Tänze f.d. Apollo Saale,* Op. 31) and familiar through the works of the Strausses, Lanner, and Gung'l. Ternary form is, as we shall see presently, even the basis of the larger forms evolved by Chopin: the scherzo, the impromptu, and the ballade.

But, admitting the primitive nature of Chopin's basic conception of form, one can have nothing but praise for the skill with which he so often modifies, adapts, or even completely conceals this naïve basis. We have already seen something of this in the great C minor Étude, Op. 10, No. 12. And we have already noticed in the Mazurka, Op. 68, No. 3, and the posthumously published Valse in E minor the 'perspective foreshortening' of the return to the first section. This curtailing of the third section of the ABA form became the rule rather than the exception with Chopin, and it is interesting to note how the same proportion of

† From *Chopin's Musical Style,* London, 1960, pp. 44–48, 72–73, 76–77, 94. Reprinted by permission of the publisher, Oxford University Press.

third section is retained even in some of the most drastically curtailed instances; for instance, in the Prelude in B minor, Op. 28, No. 6, this third section consists of four out of the twenty-six bars of the whole piece, in the Mazurka in the same key, Op. 33, No. 4, of thirty-two bars out of two hundred and twenty-odd, in the C sharp minor Nocturne, Op. 27, No. 1, of eighteen bars out of just over a hundred: that is, in each case, of about a sixth of the whole piece. The same proportion is felt again in the C minor Polonaise, Op. 40, No. 2, which is in a sort of compound ternary form with the last two sections amputated: ABA CDC A.

Chopin often offers some sort of compensation for this curtailment; he does not trust solely to one's sense of perspective to restore the balance. In the Polonaise just mentioned he takes a little three-note motive, E flat, C, B flat (which may or may not have been derived from the principal theme of the piece, but which at any rate was utterly insignificant when it appeared before in a parallel passage), builds it up for four bars to a climactic point marked by the actual return of the first theme, and then accompanies that theme with a motive derived from the E flat-C-B flat idea. The object is not merely to conceal the join, which is done quite skilfully, but to give additional weight and breadth to an architectural section that has been robbed of a good deal of length.

In other cases, for instance the C sharp minor Nocturne and the D flat Prelude, the compensation takes the form of a new idea introduced in the coda: in the former, one of astonishing freshness and beauty. Chopin's codas are often memorable as perfect roundings off of perfect poems, but, as here, they not infrequently have a structural function as well. (On the other hand, his introductions are seldom important structurally; they serve only to attract attention, or in his later works, more subtly, to place a harmonic curtain before the tonic key and so heighten the effect of its first appearance.) [1] In one piece, the B major Nocturne, Op. 32, No. 1, the extremely dramatic coda entirely takes the place of a repeat of the first section. At the end of the middle portion, which is actually related to the first by its stretto cadences, the music glides down to a dominant seventh which is succeeded, not by the expected tonic chord and opening theme, but by a foreign chord, drumlike throbs, and a tragic recitative: perhaps the most Wagnerian of all the numerous passages in which Chopin anticipates Wagner.

[1] See, for instance, the Mazurka, Op. 30, No. 4, the Scherzo in C sharp minor, and the Sonata in B flat minor, all written on the very eve of the third period. There were plenty of classical precedents for the use of this tonal curtain, but the Viennese masters rarely employed it with Chopin's subtlety.

In the B flat Prelude, Op. 28, No. 21, the repeat is not drastically replaced by an entirely new element as in this nocturne; but only the chromatic accompaniment figure returns, now in its own independent right, rises to a climax (the peak of the whole Prelude), dies down in a passage exactly parallel to one in the early part, but now entirely changed in significance, and spontaneously generates a new coda figure. The piece is one of the finest examples of Chopin's formal art on the tiny scale, for the rudimentary ternary form is completely transfigured.

"Significant line," something between melody and passage-work, but originating in embroidery of a harmonic background, played an ever more and more important part in Chopin's music in what I have called his third period. But there are naturally a number of instances in late second-period works. The first section of the Impromptu in A flat, the finale of the B flat minor Sonata, the F minor Étude, Op. 25, No. 2, the Preludes in B major, E flat minor, and B flat minor—practically all eve-of-third-period works, dating from 1838–9—are symptomatic. From the familiar broken-chord technique of the Viennese classical period, Chopin here evolves infinitely more subtle effects through thinking in terms of more advanced, chromatically complicated harmony and by the free weaving in of passing notes, ornaments, and even ornaments-to-ornaments (e.g., *acciaccature* before notes that are themselves not true harmony notes). With Mozart and Hummel even the more complicated forms of broken chord, with chromatic apoggiature and other modifications, remain unmistakably harmonic and 'passage'-like. It remained for the mature Chopin to give this type of formation linear significance and thematic importance.

Indeed he possessed a fertility in the invention of pianistic devices so inexhaustible that, a few favourite formulae apart, hardly any two pieces seem to be laid out in the same way.

In all this, of course, one sees the exuberance of the virtuoso working with absolute ease in his own peculiar medium. If the inspiration did not actually come first from the fingers, at least it must have come from fingers and brain simultaneously working in closest collaboration. It is impossible to hear such pieces as the Preludes in F sharp minor and F major, and not to realize the creative impulse that Chopin drew from the very feeling of his hands on the keyboard—the keyboard, be it remembered, not of our modern concert grand with its heavy touch and iron resonance, but of the old-fashioned 'square' piano with its simpler mechanism, lighter touch, and thinner tone.[2]

There can be little doubt, I think, that Chopin's harmony—the most important, most individual, and most fascinating of all aspects of his music—was also largely inspired, or at any rate discovered, in the same way: by improvisation at the keyboard. There may have been precedents for some of his harmonic exploits, notably in Spohr, but it is obvious that many of them were directly inspired by the timbre of the instrument or brought to light by the improviser's delicate fingers. And this is all the more important since even Chopin's basic ideas are frequently harmonic rather than melodic.

The frequency of interdominants in itself prepares the ear to accept without question the appearance of foreign chords in a key. Sometimes, instead of flying off at a tangent, Chopin omits the expected resolution of the interdominant altogether; the famous penultimate bar of the F major Prelude contains an interdominant to the subdominant triad— which is then omitted.

[2] Although Chopin's preferred instrument was a straight-strung Pleyel grand piano, 6′8″ in length and more powerful than any square, the accuracy of the author's insight is little diminished. [*Editor*]

LEONARD B. MEYER

[*Prelude No. 2*] †

Chopin's Prelude, Op. 28, No. 2 presents a clear example of the establishment of a process, its continuation, a disturbance, and, finally, the re-
establishment of a variation of the original process. The melodic phrase
(Ex. 1) consists of two similar motives joined by the fact that the same

Ex. 1

tone begins the second fragment as ended the first. The first and second
phrases are similarly linked by a common tone, though the second
phrase is displaced by an octave (Ex. 2). This process of conjunction by

Ex. 2

common tone establishes a strong force toward continuation. We expect
the next phrase, even if it involves new melodic materials, to begin with
such a tone conjunction. But this does not take place. The continuity is
broken in measure 14 by the entrance of the A where F-sharp would have
been the expected tone (Ex. 3).

† From *Emotion and Meaning in Music,* Chicago, 1956, pp. 93–97. Reprinted by
permission of the University of Chicago Press.

76

Ex. 3

break

The force of this break is not completely apparent until the motive is completed on the F-natural, since the A to E progression might simply be taken to be a repetition of the end of the second phrase. The F-natural enforces the effect of the break because, following the E, it introduces the first half step in the melody. After this break in continuity, the original process of progression by tone conjunction is re-established and, with some modifications as to motivic order, continues until the final cadential formula is reached.

The melodic break which occurs in measures 14 through 16 is paralleled by a break and change in harmonic process, but with this difference: the harmonic change is conclusive, in the sense that the old process is not re-established as was the case with the melody. Without presenting a detailed harmonic analysis of the Prelude, it is clear that the harmonic motion of the first sixteen measures might be symbolized as in Ex. 4.

Ex. 4

Although the opening phrase is originally heard in E minor, for the sake of simplicity it has been symbolized in terms of G, to which it moves. The second phrase, which seems to be exactly parallel to the first, leads us to expect a D major chord at its conclusion. But this harmony never materializes. Instead there is an irregular resolution to an altered chord, whose root must be considered as being D altered to D-sharp. Here the process changes and the change is, so to speak, suspended during the progressive alteration of this chord until the augmented sixth chord in the last half of measure 14 is reached. The irregular and indecisive character of the harmonic motion gives rise to feelings of ambiguity and uncertainty, which are resolved by the relatively clear and regular cadence from measure 14 to 15, in which the augmented sixth chord (still an alteration of the harmony which should have been D major) moves to the tonic 6/4 in A minor.

One of the most striking things about this progression is that if the sequence continued in the regular manner, with an alteration to minor at the end of the phrase, the same harmonic spot might have been reached with only minimal deviation; that is, beginning with the second phrase, we would have had the following progression:

$$D: \text{(IV)—VI—I}^6_4\text{—V—I}$$
$$A: \text{(IV)—VI—I}^6_4\text{—V—I (a minor)}$$

It seems perfectly clear that any technical explanations of measures 12 to 16 purely in terms of harmonic goals and modulations must be inadequate, since the same goal could have been reached in a much more regular way. The explanation lies in the importance of doubt and un-certainty in the shaping of aesthetic affective experience.

It is important to realize that certainty and doubt are relative terms. The beginning phrases of this Prelude are only relatively certain, particu-larly if we consider the stylistic content in which it should be heard and its relation to the preludes which precede and follow it. The constant use of non-harmonic tones and added sixths, etc., in the accompaniment figure together with the over-all subdominant progression (G to D to A) produce a feeling of indefinite tension, a kind of relative uncertainty, from the very beginning. The relative uncertainty moves to much more striking and forceful uncertainty in measure 10, where it is, in turn, resolved to a relative certainty in the arrival of the A minor 6/4 harmony. Complete certainty, toward which the piece progresses from the begin-ning, is achieved only with the final cadence, the propriety of which is apparent from this analysis.

Intensity is maintained to the end by the delay in the resolution of the 6/4 chord on A minor. Notice that while, from one point of view, the harmonic process is discontinued, from another point of view, the whole motion from measure 12 to the end is at least similar to the original process, though much prolonged:

$$a: \text{IV}^6_{4\sharp\atop 3\sharp}\text{—IV}^{6\sharp}_3\text{—(VI, omitted)—I}^6_4\text{ (prolonged)—V—V of V—V—I}$$

This example is interesting from several points of view. First, it does not have a beginning in the sense that there is no statement but only a motion and a conclusion. In this respect it is reminiscent of Wertheimer's description of the thinking processes in which we have ". . . . .S_1. . . . .S_2. . . . ."; that is, the opening phrase (S_1) is already part of a process, though in this case the final cadence does represent a final solution. Beginning during a process also contributes to the general aura of vagueness that pervades the whole Prelude. Second, this piece illustrates the difference between discontinuity through a change of process (in the harmonic motion) and discontinuity through a delay and break in a process (in the melodic motion) which is subsequently resumed. Finally, the example is noteworthy because the reversal of process and the break in melodic continuity which constitute the climax do not occur as the result of the typically rising progression but take place, so to speak, in the course of a gradually descending progression.

CHARLES BURKHART

The Polyphonic Melodic Line of Chopin's B-minor Prelude

The sixth prelude of Chopin's Op. 28 is one of those rare pieces in the piano repertory in which the melody lies chiefly in the left hand. (One thinks also of the same composer's far more complex C-sharp minor Étude.) In such pieces the left-hand part usually does double duty by consisting not only of a bass voice but also of stepwise-related tones that lie a considerable distance above the bass. That is, it will be a compound, or polyphonic, melodic line, a type of line of which Bach's suites for un-accompanied violin furnish so many obvious examples. The right-hand part of such pieces will be an accompaniment, but not of the usual kind, for it can provide no bass. On the contrary, since it is actually the highest part, it will have to form a cohesive topmost line however much over-shadowed by the melody beneath it. In sum, the composer must give the impression that the hands' roles have been exchanged, but achieve this im-pression within a tonal system whose outer-voice functions cannot actually be exchanged. The poignant B-minor Prelude is a masterly example of such an achievement, and one that we may examine more closely in terms of what happens to the melody as it passes from register to register.

The polyphonic character of the melody is established at the outset by the opening B constituting the bass voice and the d^1—$c\sharp^1$—b of mm. 1–2 the melody's upper tones. (I do not denigrate the remaining sixteenth notes of the first beat—on the contrary, I find this upward arpeggiation on a strong beat to a climax on a weak a most striking motivic idea—but pass over them because of their minimal voice-leading role.) From mm. 1 to 6 a two-measure pattern is stated three times. If one now casually hums the melody by memory from this point on, it may come as an amusing shock to discover that one is no longer humming the left-hand part. Reference to mm. 7 and 8 will reveal that indeed the hands have temporarily taken on their usual roles, and that Chopin signals this exchange by specially slurring the right-hand part over precisely these two measures plus upbeat. At this surprising change of register we note that the melody is no longer providing the bass, but that at the upbeat to m. 8 an independent bass line enters with the note d that moves to the semi-cadential V chord at the end of the first large phrase (mm. 1–8). We also note that the melody's c♯² in m. 8 (made possible by its rise into the higher octave) has the advantage of relating all the right-hand d¹'s to the semi-cadence in the most cohesive possible way. At the very point where the cadence occurs (m. 8, 2nd beat), the original register reasserts itself as the normal carrier of the melody by means of the two tones d¹–c♯¹ that proceed in untypical parallel octaves with the top! Immediately following—on the third beat—the left hand, as though hastening to snatch back its melodic role, echoes these semi-cadential top-voice tones in the *bass* register.

The melody now exactly repeats the rhythmic figure of m. 7 in mm. 15–16 and, as before, it does so in a register other than the normal one. In m. 7, however, it had lain an octave higher than normal, and here it is an octave lower. Again the register change signals an approaching cadence, but just before it occurs, the melody falls in m. 17 still another octave (e–d to D–E), then, once again abandoning its polyphonic character (as it also had done in the first phrase), takes on an exclusively bass function with the full-cadential tones F♯–B¹ of m. 17 and (after the deceptive cadence) mm. 21–22. Besides all these parallelisms with the earlier cadence (and still another will be mentioned below), we also note that this final registral plunge makes a connection with the low C♮ of m. 13. As shown in Example 1, the C♮ is the beginning of a long, stepwise bass motion that passes up to the G of the deceptive cadence at m. 18

before reaching the inevitable F♯–B¹ of mm. 21–22. Can it be irrelevant to this long-range connection that the only two bass tones under which Chopin has placed a pedal mark are this C♮ and the B¹? [1]

Ex. 1

After this dramatic excursion into the lowest register of the piece, the repetition of the opening two measures reaffirms the melody's polyphonic character.

In the forgoing I have described the course of those tones that a performer would most naturally bring out and have called these tones the "melody." In so doing I have tried to distinguish between the concepts of "melody" and "voice," finding the melody in this prelude composed principally of two voices. But not only is the melody polyphonic; the entire composition is polyphonic, the melody being just one strand. If we leave the melody severed from the whole, we will end with a distorted view of the melody and no view at all of the total work.

Example 2a shows something of the larger polyphonic organism out of which the melody flows. To achieve a clearer picture, I have removed many elaborative details of both pitch and rhythm. The large notes are those of the melody, its bass indicated by downward stems and its top tones by upward. The small, unstemmed notes show the outlines of the other voices. It will be noticed that the melody's upper tones are frequently tones which have been present in the accompaniment immediately before occurring in the melody, e.g., the d¹ in m. 1. The figure also singles out by means of brackets (⌐‾‾‾¬) a falling three-note motive that occurs in many rhythmic guises throughout the piece, often, but not exclusively, in the melody. A particularly expressive one of these is in the topmost voice at mm. 22–23: The space of a fourth rather than a third must here be spanned, but in only three notes if the motive is to be

---

[1] The melody's cadence in mm. 21–22 on purely bass-function tones recalls similar cadences in many operatic arias for the bass voice. An example is Sarastro's aria from *The Magic Flute,* "In diesen heil'gen Hallen," in which the singer's last seven measures consist almost exclusively of bass-line pitches. At the cadence, the woodwinds effect the top-line closure.

suggested. This accounts for the unusual incomplete passing tone on a^1. Another motivic parallel, shown in Example 2b, is the ingenious horizontalization in mm. 16–17 of vertical events in mm. 7–8. Both these

Ex. 2

spots are also hemiolas (see Ex. 2a), a significant rhythmic detail of the piece. We note that both occur in connection with the cadence of an eight-measure phrase—the first covering exactly the last two bars of the phrase, but the second covering the penultimate and antepenultimate bars, as in the standard late Baroque hemiola. Therefore both conclude on a cadential V chord with the melodic progression *D–C-sharp* in one of the upper voices.

Returning to the character of the melodic line, we must make a further distinction—that between changes of register that are produced (1) by the melody's merely moving from the bass voice to the top voice (as in m. 1 it moves from the bass B to the top-voice d¹) and (2) by a *single* voice moving from one octave to another. Only the second of these is properly termed " change (or, transfer) of register." (Semantically unfortunate, this term can obscure what it is supposed to clarify. It is the *voice* that is being transferred, not the register. The registers always stand still!) A vivid illustration of this technique is in the four chords that conclude the second movement of Beethoven's Piano Sonata, Op. 14, No. 2 (Ex. 3).

Ex. 3

While these changes of register are, of course, indispensable to the composition and brilliantly sum up in a final stroke the registral span of the top voice throughout the movement, it is obvious that the structure of the top voice is simply the descending scale segment F–E–D–C. Does the B-minor Prelude exhibit similar transfers? For example, does the melody's rise noted at m. 7, involve *two* voices—a middle and a top one— or basically just one voice? To clarify this and similar places, and also to uncover some additional large-scale relationships in what I consider to be the work's essential structure, I offer the following series of examples: Example 4, whose three systems—a, b, and c—are aligned to show comparable events one over the other, is a further reduction of the piece. Lines a and b, which show phrases 1 and 2 respectively, confine the essential top voice of the piece to the literal top register exclusively and the bass voice to a single low register. They show a normal voicing from which the "abnormal" voicing of the composition itself may be said to derive. Line c shows phrase 2 again, but with the top voice in the registers it actually occupies in the composition and with the other voices shifted accordingly. The top voice of line a in Example 4 illustrates my view that a true change of register does in fact occur at mm. 6–7 of the composition —that the top tones of the melody here represent just one essential voice in the structure. Lines a and b show a further close parallelism between mm. 7–8 and 15–17 (see also Ex. 2). Mm. 15–17 of line c show how the composition redistributes the voices of mm. 7–8 in the manner of invertible counterpoint. But Example 4 does not show the structure beyond the chord-to-chord voice leading. In Example 5, I submit my view of the

Ex. 4

a) Phrase 1

b) Phrase 2

c) Phrase 2 with "top" voice in the middle, then in the bass, and again in the middle register

overall harmonic structure of which these chords are an outgrowth. (Perhaps it is gratuitous to warn that the more all-embracing the generalization, the farther we are removed from the composition. I do not present Example 5 as the essence of the *music*. It is but the framework on which the music is composed. Of course, if a framework is accurately perceived, it can illumine the myriad compositional details based upon it.)

I read a long prolongation of the tonic chord from m. 1 through the I⁶ in m. 7. It embraces the VI–II♯⁷–VII♯⁶₅ of mm. 5 through 7, first beat. The fundamental top line starts on d¹ and moves to c♯¹ by m. 8. This simple motion is elaborated through (1) an upward arpeggiation from d¹ to f♯¹, then (2) a stepwise fall back to the d¹. After the semi-cadence the structure "starts over" with d¹ again in the top voice, and this time traverses its course completely: d¹–c♯¹–b. As before, the move from d¹ to c♯¹ is elaborated, not by a rise to f♯¹ but only to e¹ (mm. 12–16) which

Ex. 5

then falls through a passing tone d¹ to arrive at c♯¹ in m. 17. The e¹ is supported by the "Neapolitan" II. In my opinion, this chord is a large ♮II⁶ on the highest structural level. Why not read it, together with the subsequent VII³₄, within a large prolonged tonic that reaches from the start of the second phrase (m. 9) through the I⁶ in m. 15? In other words, why not find here another large tonic comparable to that of mm. 1–7, one that is even prolonged in a very similar manner? Because of the register of the low C♮ in mm. 13–14 which, to my ear, does *not* progress to C♯ transferred up two octaves (the c♯¹ of m. 15), but, rather, connects with m. 17's E (the third of the ♮II chord), where a small passing IV⁷ results. In support of this notion, notice the g¹ of m. 16, third beat: it contributes to a G-major chord—there is no I⁶ here as in m. 15—that likewise relates back to the ♮II. The parenthesized right-hand chords in Example 5a, mm. 15–16, then, are structurally subordinate to the ♮II^6 of the large progression I–♮II^6–V–I.[2]

Finally, the play of register in the bass voice and the bass's relation to register in the upper voices deserve special comment. The first of a long series of bass relationships that will eventually culminate in the transfer of the tonic B down one octave is occasioned by the G of m. 5. The sixth degree of the minor mode tends most naturally to resolve down one half step, but here the G is prevented from resolving to F♯ in the first phrase (mm. 1–8), which cadences on f♯ instead, thus causing a long-range "unresolved" major seventh, G–f♯. We note in passing that this G relates here as a VI to the subsequent II of m. 6, a II that brings a c♯^{2} in the topmost voice. When the G reoccurs in m. 11, its immediate function is as a dominant to the lowered II, but the pitch G itself is, on the largest level, still unresolved. The C♮ now opens up the lowest register, as we have noted. While this register is not returned to for several measures, the ♮II immediately begins to affect register in the upper voices by means of the pitch of c♮^{2}, which, *unlike* the c♯^{2} of m. 6, must press down through b^1 to a♯^{1} (mm. 15–17). Moving in parallel sixths with this voice will be the tones e^1–d^1–c♯^{1}, which threaten to collide with the e^1 reached by the melody in m. 14. Therefore the melody moves an octave lower at m. 15. The unresolved G again reasserts itself at the deceptive cadence in m. 18, almost as though the preceding F♯ (m. 17) were a passing tone, then connects with the crucial sixteenth-note

---

[2] I am indebted to Heinrich Schenker for this admittedly speculative but, I feel, insightful interpretation of the lowered II chord. Schenker's unpublished analysis of the B-minor Prelude is owned by Ernst Oster of New York City. This document, in Schenker's late style of analytic notation, but with relatively few indications of motivic parallelisms and with no commentary, will be published and fully commented upon at a later date. My analysis does not attempt to reconstruct Schenker's, but in general it employs, needless to say, many aspects of his method.

Schenker reads the fundamental top line (*Urlinie*) of the Prelude as $\hat{3}$–$\hat{2}$–$\hat{1}$, but starting from d^2 rather than d^1. On the remotest background level this difference may be insignificant. A $\hat{3}$–$\hat{2}$–$\hat{1}$ top line, it seems to me, must carry with it some form of an obligatory inner-voice line of 8–7–8, a line which will become significant on the structural level only to the degree that it is "composed out." In the Prelude I read the top voice $\hat{3}$–$\hat{2}$–$\hat{1}$ as "moved down" to an inner register (in spite of the d^2–c♯^{2} of the first phrase), an operation which leaves 8–7–8 as the actual highest voice. Once this compositional inversion is understood, reading the ultimate top line from d^1 or d^2 comes to much the same thing. I have placed it in the lower register to reflect the composition more closely.

G in m. 21 (note the right-hand chord!), and only then resolves at last to F♯. It is precisely the drop in the melody from e–d to D–E that on the immediate level has brought the F♯ here. And, of course, the D forms a long stepwise link, as we have seen, with the earlier C♮. And that C♮, when it had occurred in m. 13, had also produced an unresolved long-range major seventh with the B of bars 1 and 9 that, like the G–f♯, also demands resolution. The full cadence at m. 22 yields the resolving B¹. Example 6 summarizes this series of register-determining relationships.

Ex. 6

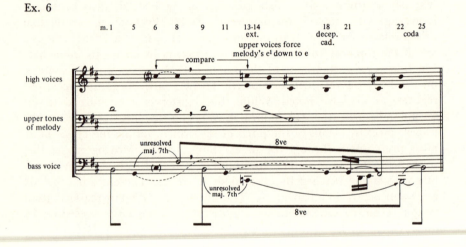

The C♮ has had long to wait before its resolution in m. 22. Small wonder that its single occurrence was stretched out for two measures and intensified with the pedal. But more, the gaining of this particular register—that is, of m. 13's C♮ rather than merely the c♮ of m. 12—even impinges on the domain of the large rhythmic structure of the prelude. For given the repetition in mm. 11–12 of the two-measure shape of 9–10, the C♮ cannot arrive until m. 13. Thus its appearance here causes the two-measure extension of the four-measure unit, 9–12. Similarly, the coda's extending of the closing tonic chord provides, among many other virtues, time for the poetic return of the opening registers.

VIEWS AND COMMENTS

ROBERT SCHUMANN†

The Preludes are strange pieces. I confess I imagined them differently, and designed in the grandest style, like his Etudes. But almost the opposite is true: they are sketches, beginnings of Etudes, or, so to speak, ruins, eagle wings, a wild motley of pieces. But each piece, written in a fine, pearly hand, shows: "Frederick Chopin wrote it." One recognizes him in the pauses by the passionate breathing. He is and remains the boldest and proudest poetic mind of the time. The collection also contains the morbid, the feverish, the repellent. May each search what suits him; may only the philistine stay away! What is a philistine?

Ein hohler Darm	[Hollow bowels
Von Furcht und Hoffnung ausgefüllt,	filled with fear and hope,
Dass Gott erbarm!	May God have mercy!]

Let us conclude, soothingly, with these beautiful lines by Schiller:

Jenes Gesetz, das mit ehernem Stab den Sträubenden lenket,
Dir nicht gilt's. Was du thust, was dir gefällt, ist Gesetz.[1]

[That law, that guides with iron rod the recalcitrant, It is not for thee. What thou doest, what pleases thee—is law.]

FRANZ LISZT *

Chopin's Preludes are compositions of an order entirely apart: they are not merely, as the title would indicate, introductions to other

---

† From *Neue Zeitschrift für Musik,* Nov. 19, 1839, No. 41, 163. Translated by Edward Lowinsky.

[1] From the poem *Der Genius,* 1795.

* From "M. Chopin The Pianiste" in *The Musical World,* June 10, 1841. This was a translation of the review by Liszt in *Revue et Gazette Musicale,* May 2, 1841, of a concert given by Chopin in Pleyel's rooms on April 26, 1841.

morceaux—they are preludes instinct with poesy, analogous to those of another great contemporary poet, who cradles the soul in golden dreams, and elevates it to the regions of the ideal. Admirable for their variety, the labour and learning with which they abound are appreciable only by the aid of a scrupulous examination; everything seems fresh, elastic, created at the impulse of the moment, abounding with that freedom of expression which is characteristic of works of genius.

HIPPOLYTE BARBEDETTE [†]

The Preludes of Chopin have, in my opinion, a greater artistic value than the Études. In them the individuality of the artist's plan is even clearer. It is difficult to present an analysis of these charming pieces, in general, little developed, some no more than a few lines, the longest two or three pages. They are very spontaneous musical outpourings. One might say that in his Preludes Chopin is complete—one of his most intimate and original works, a jewel-box of precious stones. . . .

I will speak of Chopin's general influence on modern pianists. . . . I do not hesitate to say it will be dangerous. Chopin was a sick man who enjoyed suffering, and did not want to be cured. He poured out his pain in adorable accents—this sweet melancholy language which he invented to express his sadness. One feels it irresistible and is suddenly willess before its charm; since music is above all a vague and inexplicit language, he who plays Chopin's music, for the little he is under the spell of such melancholy thought, will inevitably end by imagining that it is his own thought he expresses. He will really believe in suffering, along with him who knew so well how to weep. . . .

Conclusion: Chopin's music is essentially unhealthy. That is its imperfection and also its danger.

[†] From *Chopin: Essai de Critique Musicale*, Paris, 1861, pp. 33, 65–66. Translated by the editor.

FREDERICK NIECKS†

The indefinite character and form of the prelude, no doubt, determined the choice of the title which, however, does not describe the contents of this *opus*. Indeed, no one name could do so. This heterogeneous collection of pieces reminds me of nothing so much as of an artist's portfolio filled with drawings in all stages of advancement—finished and unfinished, complete and incomplete compositions, sketches and mere memoranda, all mixed indiscriminately together. The finished works were either too small or too slight to be sent into the world separately, and the right mood for developing, completing, and giving the last touch to the rest was gone, and could not be found again.

JAMES HUNEKER *

The twenty-five Preludes [1] alone would make good Chopin's claim to immortality. Such range, such vision, such humanity! All shades of feeling are divined, all depths and altitudes of passion explored. If all Chopin, all music, were to be destroyed, I should plead for the Preludes.

---

† From *Frederick Chopin as a Man and Musician*, 2 vols., London, 1888, II, pp. 254–255.
* From *Mezzotints in Modern Music*, 2nd ed., New York, 1899, pp. 171–172.
[1] Huneker included the Prelude in C-sharp minor, Op. 45. [*Editor*]

GEORGE SAND †

It was there [Majorca] he composed these most beautiful of short pages which he modestly entitled the Preludes. They are masterpieces. Several bring to mind visions of deceased monks and the sound of funeral chants; others are melancholy and fragrant; they came to him in times of sun and health, in the clamor of laughing children under the window, the faraway sound of guitars, birdsongs from the moist leaves, in the sight of the small pale roses coming in bloom on the snow.

Still others are of a mournful sadness, and while charming your ear, they break your heart. There is one that came to him through an evening of dismal rain—it casts the soul into a terrible dejection. Maurice and I had left him in good health one morning to go shopping in Palma for things we needed at our "encampment." The rain came in overflowing torrents. We made three leagues in six hours, only to return in the middle of a flood. We got back in absolute dark, shoeless, having been abandoned by our driver to cross unheard of perils. We hurried, knowing how our sick one would worry. Indeed he had, but now was as though congealed in a kind of quiet desperation, and, weeping, he was playing his wonderful Prelude. Seeing us come in, he got up with a cry, then said with a bewildered air and a strange tone, "Ah, I was sure that you were dead."

When he recovered his spirits and saw the state we were in, he was ill, picturing the dangers we had been through, but he confessed to me that while waiting for us he had seen it all in a dream, and no longer distinguishing the dream from reality, he became calm and drowsy while playing the piano, persuaded that he was dead himself. He saw himself drowned in a lake. Heavy drops of icy water fell in a regular rhythm on his breast, and when I made him listen to the sound of the drops of water indeed falling in rhythm on the roof, he denied having heard it. He was even angry that I should interpret this in terms of imitative sounds. He protested with all his might—and he was right to—against the childishness of such aural imitations. His genius was filled with the mysterious

† From *Histoire de Ma Vie*, 5 vols., Paris, 1902–04, IV, pp. 439–40. Translated by the editor.

sounds of nature, but transformed into sublime equivalents in musical thought, and not through slavish imitation of the actual external sounds. His composition of that night was surely filled with raindrops, resounding clearly on the tiles of the Charterhouse, but it had been transformed in his imagination and in his song into tears falling upon his heart from the sky. . . .

The gift of Chopin is [the expression of] the deepest and fullest feelings and emotions that have ever existed. He made a single instrument speak a language of infinity. He could often sum up, in ten lines that a child could play, poems of a boundless exaltation, dramas of unequalled power. . . . Mozart alone is greater, because Mozart had, besides, the composure of health and therefore the wholeness of life.

MARCEL PROUST†

When [the pianist] . . . had begun a Prelude by Chopin, Mme. de Cambremer turned to Mme. de Franquetot with a tender smile, full of intimate reminiscence, as well as of satisfaction (that of a competent judge) with the performance. She had been taught in her girlhood to fondle and cherish those long-necked, sinuous creatures, the phrases of Chopin, so free, so flexible, so tactile, which begin by seeking their ultimate resting-place somewhere beyond and far wide of the direction in which they started, the point which one might have expected them to reach, phrases which divert themselves in those fantastic bypaths only to return more deliberately—with a more premeditated reaction, with more precision, as on a crystal bowl which, if you strike it, will ring and throb until you cry aloud in anguish—to clutch at one's heart.

† From *Remembrance of Things Past,* 2 vols., transl. C. K. Scott Moncrieff, New York, 1934, I, *Swann's Way,* p. 254, with permission of the publisher, Random House, Inc.

ANDRÉ GIDE[†]

I admit that I do not understand the title that Chopin liked to give to these short *pieces:* Preludes. Preludes to what? Each of Bach's preludes is followed by its fugue; it is an integral part of it. But I find it hardly easier to imagine any one of these Preludes of Chopin followed by any other piece in the same key, be it by the same author, than all of these Preludes of Chopin played immediately one after the other. Each one of them is a prelude to a meditation; nothing can be less a concert piece; nowhere has Chopin revealed himself more intimately. Each of them, or almost (and some of them are extremely short), creates a particular atmosphere, establishes an emotional setting, then *fades out as a bird alights. All is still.*

Not all are of equal importance. Some are charming, others terrifying. None are indifferent.

[Prelude No. 1] Like the first prelude of Bach's *Clavichord,* it offers at the start a very pure phrase, which develops fully only after taking a new breath. A first impulsion forms a perfect unit, or four measures in Bach, of eight measures in Chopin, and returns to the starting-point; then takes off anew for a more complete prize whose possibility was merely indicated by the first departure.

[Prelude No. 2] Oh! no, indeed, this is not a concert piece. I can not see any audience liking it. But played in a whisper for oneself alone, its definable emotion can not be exhausted, nor that kind of almost physical terror, as if one were before a world glimpsed in passing, of a world hostile to tenderness, from which human affection is excluded.

In the *Prelude in D Minor,* the last of the collection, there likewise breathes this inexorable fatality. Dizzily remote notes are bound together by immense leaps. Here, in the melodic part too, no gentleness, but a reflection of that inexorability which the brutal bass accentuates hideously, so to speak.

† From *Notes on Chopin,* transl. by Bernard Frechtman, New York, 1949, pp. 32–33, 34–35, 46, 48–50, 79–82, 83–84. Reprinted by permission of the Philosophical Library.

I have elsewhere strongly protested against that reputation for nostalgic melancholy which is given, usually without discrimination, to all of Chopin's music, in which I have so many times encountered the expression of the highest joy. But really, in these two Preludes I find only the most sombre despair. Yes, despair; the word "melancholy" is no longer pertinent here; a feeling of the inexorable, twice cut through, in the last measures of the *Prelude in D minor,* by a harrowing moan [mm. 68–69], spasmodically taken up a second time in a twisted, jolted and, as it were, sobbing rhythm; then swept by the implacable final run, which concludes *fortissimo* in frightful depths where one touches the floor of Hell.

[Prelude No. 17] The singing voice is, at the beginning, barely distinguishable; it remains deeply involved, as if drifting in the regular flow of the six eighth-notes, where beats an impersonal heart. It happens more often than the performer, the better to stress his own emotion, thinks it necessary to give fever to that quiet pulse, which, on the contrary, I like perfectly regular.

I like the melody to take wing in a quite natural way, as if one had been expecting it to bloom; at least at the beginning of the work, for once it has spread out, the melody bursts forth and definitely takes the upper hand, to vanish away and be once again reabsorbed only toward the end. I like it to seem once again to melt into the atmosphere

> *et la voix qui chantait*
> *S'éteint comme un oiseau se pose.*
> *Tout se tait.*

> (and the voice that sang
> Dies away as a bird alights. All is silent.)

Indeed, in this Prelude, on two occasions, in the two modulations into sharp keys, Chopin attains the height of joy. And I am glad to cite these modulations, among so many others, as examples of that intense state in which joy is quite close to tears. "Oh heart grieved with joy," said Musset's Lorenzaccio.

There are, in Chopin's work, many passages more powerful, there are none in which joy takes on a more tender, more confident and purer accent. All is lost if, in this modulation into E major, the accent becomes triumphant. I want there an uncertain delight, full of astonishment, of surprise. Still more mysterious in the re-entry in F sharp major which follows immediately the one in E. The heart can not bear so much joy;

it yields, and once the supreme note has been achieved, the B, as if attained beyond all hope, the joy subsides. This B itself has nothing triumphal about it, and after the crescendo of the lower part, should be rendered only with a fading force.

[Prelude No. 23] There is a certain envelopment by the musical phrase, a certain taking possession of the listener, a certain "let-yourself-be-led" which I have never achieved, or even sought, by any pianist. They are satisfied with presenting the selection; their playing neither explains it nor develops it nor allows it to be discovered. I dictated a few pages about this matter yesterday, which, when I reread them, seemed to me good. But I would like to say a good deal more about it— to speak in particular about that false grace, that affectation (delay of the upper note which has been unexpectedly flatted—in order for expectation to be deceived, it must first be built up, be made to wait—toward the end of the Prelude in F major) which infallibly shows the tip of its camouflaged ear, there where true sensuality—rich, disturbing, indecent —is wanting.

Ah! how sure of itself the simpering grace of this pearly E flat seems to be, conscious of the effect it is going to create! (The Countess de Noailles entering a drawing-room. At last! It is She!)

T. S. ELIOT†

We have been, let us say, to hear the latest Pole
Transmit the Preludes, through his hair and finger-tips.
'So intimate, this Chopin, that I think his soul
Should be resurrected only among friends
Some two or three, who will not touch the bloom
That is rubbed and questioned in the concert room.'

† From "Portrait of a Lady," *Collected Poems 1909–1962*, New York, 1963. Reprinted by permission of Harcourt Brace Jovanovich.

KAZIMIERZ WIERZYŃSKI[†]

[Part Four from Winter Concert] [1]

Still the Preludes, almost the Pleiades,
Small silvery poppy grains falling like doves,
Will cover us, make our sight dim.
We drift, we wander out just beyond our mind
In the winter sky, on the sea, in a room, closed.
The snow clouds our eyes with a cold, wintry film.

And you can hear a comforting murmur,
And someone's love, and a girlish laughter,
And despair bursts out, out into a tear,
And a heavy silence now drifts down slowly,
And we drift on, and we drift on endlessly.
Only do not ask how or to where.

[†] From *Poezje Zebrane*, London, New York, n.d. (c. 1951).
[1] This translation of the final portion of a larger poem by Wierzyński was made by
A. Miedzyrzecki and J. Barnes.

Bibliography

Abraham, Gerald, *Chopin's Musical Style,* London, 1960.

Brown, Maurice J. E., *Chopin: An Index of His Works in Chronological Order,* London and New York, 1960.

Chomiński, Josef M., *Preludia,* Kraków, 1950.

Gide, André, *Notes on Chopin,* transl. Bernard Frechtman, New York, 1949.

Hedley, Arthur, *Chopin,* London, 1957.

Higgins, Thomas, "Chopin Interpretation" (Ph.D. dissertation, University of Iowa, 1966), University Microfilms #67–2629.

Leichtentritt, Hugo, *Analyse von Chopinschen Klavierwerken,* 2 vols., Berlin, 1921.

Meyer, Leonard B., *Emotion and Meaning in Music,* Chicago, 1956.

Niecks, Frederick, *Frederick Chopin as a Man and Musician,* 2 vols., London, 1888.

Sand, George, *Histoire de Ma Vie,* 5 vols. Paris, 1902–04.

Sydow, Bronislas Édouard, *Bibliografia F. F. Chopina.* Warszawa, 1949.

—— *Correspondance de Frédéric Chopin,* Paris, n.d.